Edexcel GCSE
Music
Practice
Listening
Papers

Teacher Book and CD

John Arkell • Jonny Martin

Edited by Julia Winterson

A PEARSON COMPANY

Published by Pearson Education Limited, a company incorporated in England and Wales, having its registered office at Edinburgh Gate, Harlow, Essex, CM20 2JE. Registered company number: 872828

www.pearsonschoolsandfecolleges.co.uk

Edexcel is a registered trademark of Edexcel Limited

Text copyright © Pearson Education Limited 2011
Layout © 2011 Hinrichsen Edition, Peters Edition Limited, London
www.editionpeters.com

Edited by Julia Winterson
Typeset by Peter Nickol
Cover design © Pearson Education Limited 2011
Printed in the United Kingdon by Ashford Colour Press Ltd, Gosport, Hampshire

First published 2011

15
10 9 8 7 6 5

British Library Cataloguing in Publication Data
A catalogue record for this book is available from the British Library.
ISBN 978 1 846908149

Extract of Grace from *Grace*.
Words and music by Jeff Buckley & Gary Lucas. © Copyright 1994 Sony/ATV Songs LLC, El Viejito Music & Gary Lucas Music, USA. Sony/ATV Music Publishing (UK) Limited (50%)/Universal/MCA Music Limited (50%). Used by permission of Music Sales Limited

Extract of *Something's coming* from West Side Story.
Words by Stephen Sondheim, music by Leonard Bernstein. © Copyright 1956, 1957, 1958, 1959 by the Estate of Leonard Bernstein and Stephen Sondheim. Copyright renewed. Leonard Bernstein Music PublishingCompany LLC, Publisher. Boosey & Hawkes, inc., Sole Agent. International Copyright Secured. Reproduced by permission of Boosey & Hawkes Music Publishers Ltd.

Extract of Yiri from *Burkina Faso: Balafons et tambours*.
Written by Madou Koné. Published by Sunset France.

Contents

Introduction

This Teacher book accompanies the Edexcel GCSE Music Practice Listening Papers A, B and C and supports Unit 3: Music – Listening and Appraising. The book contains Papers A, B and C, with the mark scheme for each question provided on the facing pages. The marking guidance on page 5 gives details of the general approach to marking the papers.

There is also a CD with the audio tracks for each paper. The mark scheme indicates which track is to be played for each question and the question paper indicates the number of times the track should be played. There is a full track listing on page 80.

Students should be given one minute's reading time at the start of each question and three minutes to complete their answers at the end of each question.

General Marking Guidance

- All candidates must receive the same treatment. Examiners must mark the first candidate in exactly the same way as they mark the last.

- Mark schemes should be applied positively. Candidates must be rewarded for what they have shown they can do rather than penalised for omissions.

- Examiners should mark according to the mark scheme not according to their perception of where the grade boundaries may lie.

- There is no ceiling on achievement. All marks on the mark scheme should be used appropriately.

- All the marks on the mark scheme are designed to be awarded. Examiners should always award full marks if deserved, i.e. if the answer matches the mark scheme. Examiners should also be prepared to award zero marks if the candidate's response is not worthy of credit according to the mark scheme.

- Where some judgement is required, mark schemes will provide the principles by which marks will be awarded and exemplification may be limited.

- When examiners are in doubt regarding the application of the mark scheme to a candidate's response, the team leader must be consulted.

- Crossed out work should be marked UNLESS the candidate has replaced it with an alternative response.

- Quality of written communication (QWC) should be taken into account in the marking of responses to the choice of Question 9 or 10. Quality of written communication includes clarity of expression, the structure and presentation of ideas and grammar, punctuation and spelling.

SECTION A

Answer all questions in this section.

Some questions must be answered with a cross in a box ☒. If you change your mind about an answer, put a line through the box ☒ and then mark your new answer with a cross ☒.

Area of Study 1
Mozart: 1ˢᵗ movement from Symphony No. 40 in G minor, K550

1 Listen to the following extract, which will be played **three** times.

(a) Which theme does Mozart use in this extract? Put a cross in the correct box.

A 1ˢᵗ Subject ☒

B 2ⁿᵈ Subject ☒

(1)

(b) Which of the following best describes the tonality at the start of the extract? Put a cross in the correct box.

A Major, with some chromatic notes ☒

B Major throughout ☒

C Minor, with some chromatic notes ☒

D Minor throughout ☒

(1)

(c) Complete the sentences, choosing the correct words from the choices given below each blank space.

At the very end of the extract, the violins, bassoons and _____ play a

|flutes| |oboes|

_____ _____ . It is performed _____ .

|rising| |falling| |scale| |arpeggio| |legato| |staccato|

(4)

(d) The extract is taken from the exposition section of this movement. Name two other sections commonly found in sonata form.

1 ....

2 ....

(2)

(Total for Question 1 = 8 marks)

Mark Scheme

Mozart	1st Movement from Symphony No. 40 in G minor	Anthology bars 44–72	CD track 1	

Question number	Correct answer	Mark
1(a)	**B** 2nd subject	1

Question number	Correct answer	Mark
1(b)	**A** Major, with some chromatic notes	1

Question number	Correct answer	Mark
1(c)	1) Flutes 2) Falling 3) Scale 4) Staccato	4

Question number	Correct answer	Mark
1(d)	Any **two** of: • Development • Recapitulation • Coda/codetta • Bridge passage	2

Area of Study 1
Chopin: Prelude No. 15 in D flat major, Op. 28

2 Listen to the following extract, which will be played **three** times.

   (a) Which section of the piece is the extract taken from?

   ....

   (1)

   (b) Complete the table below to describe the extract:

Musical Element	Description
Dynamics	1 There is a diminuendo at the beginning of the extract 2 The extract ends very quietly
Tempo	1 .... 2 .... 3 .... (3)
Texture	1 .... 2 .... (2)

   (c) What is the tonality of the extract? Put a cross in the correct box.

   A Major   ☒

   B Minor   ☒

   C Modal   ☒

   D Pentatonic   ☒

   (1)

   (d) What is the cadence at the end of the extract?

   ....

   (1)

   (e) What does the symbol 𝄢. indicate that the pianist should do?

   ....

   (1)

   (Total for Question 2 = 9 marks)

Mark Scheme

Chopin	Prelude No. 15 in D flat major	Anthology bars 81–89	CD track 2	

Question number	Correct answer		Acceptable answers	Mark
2(a)	Any **one** of • Coda • Codetta		• Tail • End • Final section	1

Question number	Correct answer	Mark
2(b)	**TEMPO** Any **three** of: • Rubato throughout • (Slight) pause on first note • Pause on each of the last few notes • Ritenuto/rallentando at end • Slow **TEXTURE** Any **two** of: • Starts with a single melody line/monophonic • Pedal missing at the beginning • Pedal returns after opening • Mostly melody and accompaniment/homophonic	5

Question number	Correct answer	Mark
2(c)	**A** Major	1

Question number	Correct answer	Acceptable answers	Mark
2(d)	Perfect	• V(7)–I • (Full) closed	1

Question number	Correct answer	Acceptable answers	Reject	Mark
2(e)	Press the sustain pedal	• Sostenuto • Loud pedal • Right pedal	Soft pedal	1

Area of Study 2
Steve Reich: 3rd movement (fast) from Electric Counterpoint

3   Listen to the following extract, which will be played **three** times.

(a) Describe what happens to the bass parts in the opening bars of the extract.

....

(2)

(b) The extract begins and ends in E minor. Which other key can be heard shortly after the start of the extract? Put a cross in the correct box.

A A minor ☒

B B major ☒

C C minor ☒

D D major ☒

(1)

(c) What is the technical term for the part played by the live performer?

....

(1)

(d) Describe the texture of the extract.

....

....

....

(2)

(e) Which **two** of the following minimalist techniques are **not** heard in the extract? Put crosses in the boxes to indicate your answers.

A Layering   ☒

B Metamorphosis ☒

C Note addition ☒

D Repetition   ☒

(2)

(Total for Question 3 = 8 marks)

Mark Scheme

Reich	3rd movement (fast) from Electric Counterpoint	Anthology bars 106–140	CD track 3	

Question number	Correct answer	Acceptable answer	Mark
3(a)	Any **two** of: • They fade away • Gradual diminuendo • To silence/nothing	They drop out/stop playing (1)	2

Question number	Correct answer	Mark
3(b)	**C** C minor	1

Question number	Correct answer	Reject	Mark
3(c)	Resultant (melody)	Live part	1

Question number	Correct answer	Mark
3(d)	Any **two** of: • Starts with many parts and thins out almost immediately • The texture then remains the same for the rest of the extract • Layered • Thins out almost immediately (1) to five parts (1) • Imitative/canonic • Polyphonic/contrapuntal • Ends on a sustained chord	2

Question number	Correct answer	Mark
3(e)	**B** Metamorphosis **C** Note addition	2

Area of Study 2
Schoenberg: *Peripetie* from Five Orchestral Pieces, Op. 16

4 Listen to the following extracts, which will each be played **three** times.

(a) Identify **two** differences and **two** similarities between the two extracts.

Differences

1 ....

2 ....

Similarities

1 ....

2 ....

(4)

(b) List **three** instruments that play the principal melody (Hauptstimme) in **either** extract.

1 ....

2 ....

3 ....

(3)

(c) What is the tonality of the music? Put a cross in the correct box.

A Atonal   ☒

B Major   ☒

C Minor   ☒

D Pentatonic   ☒

(1)

(Total for Question 4 = 8 marks)

Mark Scheme

Schoenberg	*Peripetie* from Five Orchestral Pieces	1) bars 6–18 2) bars 37–48	CD track 4	

Question number	Correct answer	Mark
4(a)	**DIFFERENCES** Any **two** of: • Violins at very start of extract 2 • Extract 2 features a pizzicato double bass note • Melodic lines are different • First extract features bass clarinet (1) and bassoon (1) ostinato (1) • First extract features solo clarinet at end • Second extract features bassoon (1) and (solo) cello (1) at end • Any other valid point **SIMILARITIES** Any **two** of: • (French) horns play opening idea (1) in chords (1) with a homophonic texture (1) • Both extracts have quiet dynamics • Much use of dynamic shading • Much use of legato phrasing • Both feature changing solo instruments • Both atonal • Both use angular melodic lines • Both motivic • Both feature use of hexachords • Same time signature/three in a bar/triple time • Any other valid point	4

Question number	Correct answer	Acceptable answers	Mark
4(b)	Any **three** of: • (French) horn(s) • Clarinet(s) • Bassoon(s) • Cello(s)	• Violin(s) (at the very beginning of extract 2) • Trumpet(s)	3

Question number	Correct answer	Mark
4(c)	**A** Atonal	1

Area of Study 3
Jeff Buckley: *Grace* from the album Grace

5 Listen to the following extract which will be played **four** times.

(a) Look at the following melody, which is heard at the beginning of the extract. Fill in the missing notes in bar 1. The rhythm is given above the stave.

(4)

(b) Complete the table below to describe how the music reflects the tortured mood of the lyrics.

		Description
Vocal performance	1	
	2	
		(2)
How the instruments are played	1	
	2	
		(2)

(c) Near the end of the extract, the vocal sound changes on the words *it reminds me of the pain*. How has this been achieved?

....

(1)

(Total for Question 5 = 9 marks)

Mark Scheme

Jeff Buckley	*Grace*	Chorus and Bridge	CD track 5	

Question number	Correct answer	Mark
5(a)	One mark for each correct pitch	4

Question number	Correct answer	Mark
5(b)	**VOCAL PERFORMANCE** Any **two** of: • Use of falsetto • Passionate delivery • High vocal range • Strained sound of the vocals • Much use of melisma • Wordless 'cries' of anguish **HOW THE INSTRUMENTS ARE PLAYED** Any **two** of: • Electric and acoustic guitars strummed aggressively • Much use of cymbals • Many rolls around kit • Tremolo strings • Use of slides/glissandi in electric guitar	4

Question number	Correct answer	Acceptable answers	Reject	Mark
5(c)	EQ effect (high and low frequencies removed)	• Reduced bit rate • Vocoder	Telephone effect	1

Area of Study 3
Moby: *Why does my heart feel so bad* from the album Play

6 Listen to the following extract which will be played **three** times.

(a) Which section of the song is the extract taken from? Put a cross in the correct box.

  A Chorus ☒

  B Intro ☒

  C Middle 8 ☒

  D Verse ☒

(1)

(b) At the very end of the extract most of the instruments drop out. What is this section called in dance music?

....

(1)

(c) List **three** studio effects that have been applied to the vocal sample.

  1 ....

  2 ....

  3 ....

(3)

(d) Listen to the drum part.

  (i) Have the drums been performed live or have they been programmed?

  ....

(1)

  (ii) Give a musical reason for your answer.

  ....

(1)

(e) Give **two** musical reasons why you like or dislike this song.

  1 ....

  2 ....

(2)

(Total for Question 6 = 9 marks)

Mark Scheme

Moby	*Why does my heart feel so bad*	Verse before breakdown	CD track 6	

Question number	Correct answer	Mark
6(a)	**D** Verse	1

Question number	Correct answer	Mark
6(b)	Breakdown	1

Question number	Correct answer	Acceptable answers	Mark
6(c)	Any **three** of: • Delay/echo • Reverb • Compression • EQ	• Limiting • Filtering • Panning	3

Question number	Correct answer	Mark
6(d)(i)	Programmed	1
6(d)(ii)	Any valid **musical** reason. For instance: They sound rather mechanical/they are very precise/they sound electronic rather than acoustic	1

Question number	Correct answer	Mark
6(e)	Any **two musical** reasons	2

Area of Study 4
Capercaillie: *Chuir m'athair mise dhan taigh charraideach (the Skye Waulking Song)* from the album Nadurra

7 Listen to the following extract which will be played **three** times.

(a) Complete the chord sequence heard in this extract.

Bars	1	2	3	4
	C major		E minor C major	G major
Bars	**5**	**6**	**7**	**8**
	C major		E minor C major	

(3)

(b) Complete the table below, naming the two musical styles heard in the extract. Give a reason for each answer.

	Musical style	Reason
1		
2		

(4)

(c) What is the purpose of the nonsense syllables in waulking songs?

....

(1)

(Total for Question 7 = 8 marks)

Mark Scheme

Capercaillie	*Chuir m'athair mise dhan taigh charraideach (the Skye Waulking Song)*	Verse	CD track 7	

Question number	Correct answer	Mark
7(a)	Bar 2: G major Bar 6: G major Bar 8: G major	3

Question number	Correct answer	Mark
7(b)	Musical style: Celtic/Scottish/folk Reasons: • Acoustic instruments used e.g. accordion/fiddle/bouzouki – NOT uilleann pipes (not present in extract) • Lyrics in Gaelic • Waulking song is a folk song • Lilting metre • Call and response vocals • Vocal melody mostly pentatonic Style of music: (Western) popular/pop/rock Reasons: • Instruments (must be named) – drum kit, electric piano (Wurlitzer), bass guitar, NOT synth (not present in extract) • Production of recording • Electric instruments used (i.e. not exclusively acoustic) • Diatonic, simple harmony • Repetitive chord sequence One mark for each style of music and one mark for the reason given.	4

Question number	Correct answer	Mark
7(c)	Any **one** of: • Any valid response relating to work song (e.g. keeping rhythm of the work/relieves the boredom of repetitive tasks) • Gives the lead singer time to prepare the next line	1

Area of Study 4
Rag Desh

8 Listen to the following extract, which will be played **three** times.

(a) (i) Apart from the tambura, name the **two** string instruments heard in the extract.

1 ....

2 ....

(2)

(ii) Which statement describes how the instruments are played? Put a cross in the correct box.

A They are both plucked ☒

B One is plucked and one is bowed ☒

C They are both bowed ☒

(1)

(b) Name two percussion instruments heard in the extract.

1 ....

2 ....

(2)

(c) Complete the following sentence:

In Indian rag, the rhythmic cycle is called the ....

(1)

(d) Which of the following rhythmic cycles can be heard in the extract? Put a cross in the correct box.

A 7 beats: 3 + 2 + 2 ☒

B 8 beats: 2 + 2 + 2 + 2 ☒

C 10 beats: 2 + 3 + 2 + 3 ☒

D 12 beats: 2 + 2 + 2 + 2 + 2 + 2 ☒

(1)

(e) Give **two** musical reasons why this is a typical vocal performance of Indian rag.

1 ....

2 ....

(2)

(Total for Question 8 = 9 marks)

Mark Scheme

Chiranji Lal Tanwar	Rag Desh	Alap into Bhajan	CD track 8	

Question number	Correct answer	Mark
8(a)(i)	• Sarod • Sarangi	2
8(a)(ii)	**B** One is plucked and one is bowed	1

Question number	Correct answer	Mark
8(b)	Any **two** of: • Tabla • Cymbals • Pakhawaj	2

Question number	Correct answer	Mark
8(c)	Tal	1

Question number	Correct answer	Mark
8(d)	**B** 8 beats	1

Question number	Correct answer	Mark
8(e)	Any **two** of: • Highly ornamented • Improvised • Use of rag for melodic content • Any other valid point	2

SECTION B

Answer EITHER Question 9 OR Question 10

If you answer Question 9 put a cross in this box ☒.

9 The following questions are about *And the glory of the Lord* from Messiah, HWV56 by Handel.

(a) In which century was Messiah composed?

....

(1)

(b) Messiah is an example of what type of sacred choral work?

....

(1)

(c) Comment on how Handel uses the following elements in *And the glory of the Lord*.

- Melody
- Harmony and tonality
- Dynamics
- Texture
- Mood

Remember to use correct **musical vocabulary** where appropriate.

(10)

....

....

....

....

....

....

....

....

....

....

....

....

....

....

Mark Scheme

Handel	*And the glory of the Lord* from Messiah	

Question number	Correct answer	Mark
9(a)	18th century	1

Question number	Correct answer	Mark
9(b)	Oratorio	1

Question number	Indicative content
9(c) QWC i–ii–iii	**Melody** • Four main melodies • Each idea relates to a particular part of the text • One idea uses sequence • Another has a short, repeated motif • Another is made up mainly of long, repeated As • Each melodic idea is contrasting • Any other valid point **Harmony and tonality** • The tonality is major throughout • The major tonality lends the piece a bright, joyous mood • Any modulations are to the dominant (and the dominant of the dominant) • Adding to the bright feel of the piece • The piece is marked by frequent perfect cadences, reinforcing the key • The piece ends with a plagal cadence • Any other valid point **Dynamics** • The dynamics are terraced • As is common in Baroque music • The dynamics are often determined by the number of parts playing at a given point • The piece starts off quietly with the orchestral introduction • The piece ends with a dramatic rest followed by a loud cadence • Any other valid point **cont. over**

(Total for Question 9 = 12 marks)

Question number	Indicative content
9(c) cont. **QWC** **i–ii–iii**	**Texture** • The first vocal entry is monophonic • Much imitation throughout • Some doubling of parts "for the mouth of the Lord" • Homophonic for the final cadence • The texture is constantly changing • Handel sets big textural contrasts in close proximity for maximum impact • Any other valid point **Mood** • Baroque music tends to have one prevailing mood for a whole piece • Called an 'affection' • The mood is joyful • It is reinforced by the major tonality • And the sprightly tempo • And the 3/4 metre • Any other valid point

If you answer Question 10 put a cross in this box ☒.

10 The following questions are about *All blues* from the album Kind of Blue by Miles Davis.

(a) In which year was this album originally released? Put a cross in the correct box.

    A 1939   ☒

    B 1959   ☒

    C 1979   ☒

    D 1999   ☒

(1)

(b) *All blues* is an example of what style of music?

....

(1)

(c) Comment on how Miles Davis uses the following musical elements in *All blues*.

- Melody
- Harmony and tonality
- Rhythm
- Texture
- Structure

Remember to use correct **musical vocabulary** where appropriate.

(10)

....

....

....

....

....

....

....

....

....

....

....

....

....

Mark Scheme

Miles Davis	*All blues*	

Question number	Correct answer	Mark
10(a)	**B** 1959	1

Question number	Correct answer	Mark
10(b)	Jazz	1

Question number	Indicative content
10(c) **QWC** **i–ii–iii**	**Melody** • Main melody called the head • Head is slow and mostly conjunct • With the addition of the major sixth interval • There is some chromatic movement • The solos are much more free • Melodies are based on modes, scales and broken chords • As the solos progress the melodies become more complicated and virtuosic • Any other valid point **Harmony and tonality** • Modal • This album was at the forefront of modal jazz • Many seventh chords • And extended chords • Use of 7(♯9) very important to punctuate the sections • Slow harmonic motion • Some chromaticism • And dissonance • Any other valid point <div align="right">**cont. over**</div>

Question number	Indicative content
10(c) cont. **QWC** **i–ii–iii**	**Rhythm** • Swung rhythm • Compound metre • Much use of syncopation • And polyrhythms • Some rhythmic displacement to make the most of short melodic motifs • Any other valid point **Texture** • Starts with just the drum kit (played with brushes), bass and piano • Then the texture builds up as instruments are added • Saxophones enter with the chordal riff followed by the trumpet with the head • After the head, the solos have one instrument plus rhythm section • Each solo is punctuated by a link in which the texture is thinner • Any other valid point **Structure** • The basic building block is the 12-bar blues chord sequence • This is repeated 19 times in the piece • Intro • Head • Solos interspersed with 4-bar links • Head returns after the solos • Piece closes with an outro to fade • Any other valid point

Mark Scheme for Questions 9(c) and 10(c)

Level	Mark	Descriptor
Level 0	0	No positive features can be identified in the response.
Level 1	1–2 **Limited** analysing and evaluating skills	• Little relevant information regarding the question and set work(s) is conveyed. • Knowledge of key features of the set work(s) will be limited and/or incorrectly applied. • Range of musical vocabulary is limited and/or is not used correctly. • The skills needed to produce effective writing will not normally be present and answer lacks both clarity and organisation. Frequent spelling, punctuation and grammar errors will be present.
Level 2	3–4 **Basic** analysing and evaluating skills	• Some relevant information regarding the question and set work(s) is conveyed but there will be major omissions. • Knowledge of key features of the set work(s) will be basic with only the most obvious of comments made. • Range of musical vocabulary is basic but mostly used correctly. • The skills needed to produce effective writing are likely to be limited and passages within the answer will lack both clarity and organisation. Frequent spelling, punctuation and/or grammar errors will be present.
Level 3	5–6 **Competent** analysing and evaluating skills	• Relevant information regarding the question and set work(s) is conveyed but there will still be some (mostly) minor omissions. • Knowledge of key features of the set work(s) will be competent, with an adequate range of knowledge displayed. • Range of musical vocabulary is quite broad and is mostly used correctly. • Most of the skills needed to produce effective writing will be present but there will be lapses in clarity and organisation. Some spelling, punctuation and grammar errors will be present.
Level 4	7–8 **Good** analysing and evaluating skills	• Relevant information regarding the question and set work(s) is conveyed and omissions will be minor. • Knowledge of key features of the set work(s) will be good, with both range and some depth of knowledge displayed. • Range of musical vocabulary is broad and is mostly used correctly. • The skills needed to produce convincing writing are mostly in place. Good clarity and organisation. Some spelling, punctuation and grammar errors will be found but overall the writing will be coherent.
Level 5	9–10 **Excellent** analysing and evaluating skills	• Relevant information regarding the set work(s) is conveyed and any omissions are negligible. • Knowledge of key features of the set work(s) will be excellent, with a wide range and depth of knowledge displayed. • Range of music vocabulary is extensive and any errors in usage are minor. • All the skills needed to produce convincing writing are in place. Excellent clarity and organisation. Very few spelling, punctuation and/or grammar errors will be found and they will not detract from the overall coherence.

SECTION A

Answer all questions in this section.

Some questions must be answered with a cross in a box ☒. If you change your mind about an answer, put a line through the box ☒ and then mark your new answer with a cross ☒.

Area of Study 1
G.F. Handel: *And the glory of the Lord* from Messiah, HWV56

1 Listen to the following extract, which will be played **two** times.

(a) In what order do the voices enter at the start of the extract? Put a cross in the correct box.

   A Bass Tenor Alto   ☒

   B Tenor Alto Bass   ☒

   C Alto Tenor Bass   ☒

   D Bass Alto Tenor   ☒

(1)

(b) Complete the following sentences about the extract:

The soprano entry *and the glory of the Lord* is mostly sung without other voices in

a(n) .... texture.

The melody is doubled by 1ˢᵗ and 2ⁿᵈ ....s.

(2)

(c) How is the word *revealed* set to music in this chorus?

....

(1)

(d) Which of the following is true of the music of the orchestra and choir in the extract? Put a cross in the correct box.

   A The orchestra plays chords to accompany the choir parts   ☒

   B The orchestra doubles the choir parts   ☒

   C The orchestra plays in dialogue with the choir parts   ☒

   D The orchestra only plays when the choir parts have rests   ☒

(1)

(e) How is a stately and grand ending achieved in the last three bars to the words *have spoken it*?

1 ....

2 ....

(2)

Mark Scheme

Handel	*And the glory of the Lord*	Anthology bars 102–138 (end)	CD track 9	

Question number	Correct answer	Mark
1(a)	**C** Alto Tenor Bass	1

Question number	Correct answer	Acceptable answer	Mark
1(b)	1) monophonic 2) violins	1) unison	2

Question number	Correct answer	Acceptable answers	Mark
1(c)	Any **one** of • Melismatic/melisma • Made up of a sequence (of four notes) • Used in imitation	• More than one note per syllable • Counterpoint/imitation	1

Question number	Correct answer	Mark
1(d)	**B** The orchestra doubles the choir parts	1

Question number	Correct answer	Mark
1(e)	Any **two** of: • Slow/stately tempo • All voices together/homophonic texture • Loud/*forte*/*f* • Long note values/sustained notes • Same rhythm in each part • Strong plagal (amen) cadence • General Pause/GP	2

(f) In which year was this music first performed? Put a cross in the correct box.

    A 1642 ☒

    B 1742 ☒

    C 1842 ☒

    D 1942 ☒

(1)

(Total for Question = 8 marks)

Question number	Correct answer	Mark
1(f)	**B** 1742	1

Area of Study 1
Chopin: Prelude No. 15 in D flat major, Op. 28

2 Listen to the following extract, which will be played **four** times.

(a) What section of the piece is the extract from? Put a cross in the correct box.

  A A-section   ☒

  B B-section   ☒

(1)

(b) Which hand plays the melody? ....

(1)

(c) What is the tonality of the music? Put a cross in the correct box.

  A Major   ☒

  B Minor   ☒

  C Modal   ☒

  D Pentatonic   ☒

(1)

(d) What musical device is created by the repeated quaver G sharps in the extract?

....

(1)

(e) Describe the dynamics of the extract. Make two points.

  (i) ....

  (ii) ....

(2)

(f) Look at the following melody, which is heard at the beginning of the extract.

  Fill in the missing notes in bar 3. The rhythm is given above the stave.

(4)

(g) State **one** feature of Romantic piano music heard in this extract.

....

(1)

(Total for Question 2 = 11 marks)

Mark Scheme

Chopin	Prelude No. 15 in D flat major	Anthology bars 60–75	CD track 10	

Question number	Correct answer		Mark
2(a)	**B** B-section		1

Question number	Correct answer	Acceptable answers	Mark
2(b)	Right (hand)	• Treble (part) • Top	1

Question number	Correct answer	Mark
2(c)	**B** Minor	1

Question number	Correct answer	Acceptable answer	Mark
2(d)	Pedal (inner)	Ostinato	1

Question number	Correct answer	Mark
2(e)	Any **two** of: • Starts quietly/*piano*/***p*** • Some small hairpins (louder then softer) • Crescendos to loud/*forte*/***f*** • And diminuendos/then softer • Ends softly/*piano*/***p***	2

Question number	Correct answer	Mark
2(f)	 **One** mark for each correct pitch	4

Question number	Correct answer	Mark
2(g)	Any **one** of: • Expressive playing • Use of rubato • Much use of dynamic shading/crescendos and diminuendos • Expressive/sustained melody • Use of chromatic/complex chords • Much use of sustaining pedal • Rich texture	1

Area of Study 2
Bernstein: *Something's coming* from West Side Story

3   Listen to the following extract, which will be played **three** times.

   (a)   Which of the following rhythms is used in the bass line throughout the extract? Put a cross in the correct box.

(1)

   (b)   Make one comment about each of the following musical elements used in the extract:

   (i) Melody line ....

(1)

   (ii) Rhythm ....

(1)

   (c)   Describe **one** way in which anticipation and excitement are captured in the music.

   ....

(1)

   (d)   Which twentieth-century musical style has influenced the music of the song?

   ....

(1)

   (e)   Give **two musical** reasons why you like or dislike this piece of music.

   1 ....

   2 ....

(2)

(Total for Question 3 = 7 marks)

Mark Scheme

Bernstein	*Something's coming* from West Side Story	Anthology bars 40–63	CD track 11	

Question number	Correct answer	Mark
3(a)	B	1

Question number	Correct answer	Mark
3(b)	**MELODY** Any **one** of: • Short phrases (1)/2-bar phrases • Narrow range (1)/range of a 6th • Some accented notes **RHYTHM** Any **one** of: • Syncopated (1) • Some straight rhythms (1) at *something's coming* (1) • Repeated rhythmic motive (1) • Accompaniment has quavers (1) throughout (1)	2

Question number	Correct answer	Mark
3(c)	Any **one** of: • Fast tempo • Exciting syncopated rhythms • Short repeated phrases • Leading to a long/sustained note • Use of accents • Use of crescendo • The words	1

Question number	Correct answer	Mark
3(d)	Jazz	1

Question number	Acceptable answers	Mark
3(e)	Any valid **musical** answers e.g. syncopated rhythms/fast tempo, catchy melody line	2

Area of Study 2
Reich: 3rd movement (fast) from Electric Counterpoint

4   Listen to the following extract, which will be played **three** times.

(a) What style is this piece of music written in?

....

(1)

(b) Complete the following sentence, using the words given below.

        solo   *bass*   *seven*

The piece is scored for a live guitarist playing a .... part with a taped

ensemble of .... guitar parts and two .... guitars.

(3)

(c) What is the time signature of the music? Put a cross in the correct box.

   A 4/4   ☒

   B 12/8   ☒

   C 3/2   ☒

   D 6/16   ☒

(1)

(d) The first part heard in the extract is Guitar 1. Choose **two** phrases from the list below that describe this part in the opening bars.

        repeated motif   *uses minims*   *ascending pattern of notes*

        low register of guitar   *syncopated rhythm*   *strummed chords*

   1 ....

   2 ....

(2)

(e) Make **two** comments about the musical texture in the extract.

   1 ....

   2 ....

(2)

(Total for Question 4= 9 marks)

Mark Scheme

Reich	3rd movement (fast) from Electric Counterpoint	Anthology bars 1–33	CD track 12	

Question number	Correct answer	Mark
4(a)	Minimalism/minimalist	1

Question number	Correct answer	Mark
4(b)	1) Solo 2) Seven/7 3) Bass	3

Question number	Correct answer	Mark
4(c)	**C** 3/2	1

Question number	Correct answer	Mark
4(d)	• Repeated motif • Syncopated rhythm	2

Question number	Correct answer	Mark
4(e)	Any **two** of • Starts with a single/solo/monophonic line • Parts come in one at a time • Creates a layered texture • Contrapuntal • Interlocking parts/phrases • Bass parts come in last	2

Area of Study 3
Miles Davis: *All blues* from the album Kind of Blue

5 Listen to the following extract which will be played **two** times.

(a) Name the instrument playing the solo part.

....

(1)

(b) The soloist plays two 12-bar choruses. Describe **one** feature of the music played by this instrument.

....

(1)

(c) Name the **two** instruments that accompany the soloist.

Instrument 1 ....

Instrument 2 ....

(2)

(d) Complete the 12-bar chord sequence (bars 3, 6 and 9) played twice throughout the extract.

Bar 1	Bar 2	Bar 3	Bar 4
G7	**G7**		**G7**
Bar 5	Bar 6	Bar 7	Bar 8
Gm		**G7**	**G7**
Bar 9	Bar 10	Bar 11	Bar 12
	E♭7(♯9) D7(♯9)	**G7**	**G7**

(3)

(e) What musical skill is demonstrated in the music of the solo sections in *All blues*?

....

(1)

(Total for Question 5 = 8 marks)

Mark Scheme

Miles Davis	*All blues*	Anthology bars 197–220	CD track 13	

Question number	Correct answer	Mark
5(a)	Piano	1

Question number	Correct answer	Mark
5(b)	Any **one** of: <ul><li>First chorus melody in right hand part</li><li>First chorus left hand comping/plays chords</li><li>Second chorus is more chord-based solo</li><li>Some alternation of hands</li><li>Uses middle range (of keyboard) notes</li><li>Swung rhythm/syncopation, repeated motives</li></ul>	1

Question number	Correct answer	Mark
5(c)	<ul><li>Drum kit (using brushes)</li><li>String bass/double bass</li></ul> (either way round)	2

Question number	Correct answer	Mark
5(d)	Bar 3: G7 Bar 6: Gm Bar 9: D7(♯9)	3

Question number	Correct answer	Acceptable answers	Mark
5(e)	Improvised/improvisation	<ul><li>Made up</li><li>Not notated</li></ul>	1

Area of Study 3
Buckley: *Grace* from the album Grace

6 Listen to the following extract which will be played **two** times. The music features the introduction and first verse of the song.

INTRODUCTION (Bars 1 to 7)

(a) Which of the following describes the tonality of the introduction? Put a cross in the correct box.

   A Bars 1 to 3 are in no clear key whereas bars 4 to 7 are in D minor ☒

   B Bars 1 to 3 are in no clear key whereas bars 4 to 7 are in D major ☒

   C Bars 1 to 3 are in no clear key whereas bars 4 to 7 are modal ☒

   D Bars 1 to 3 are in no clear key whereas bars 4 to 7 are atonal ☒

   (1)

(b) The music of bar 1 is repeated at bar 2 a tone higher. What is this device called?

   ....

   (1)

(c) Name **two** different playing techniques used by the electric guitar in the introduction.

   1 (bars 1–3) ....

   2 (bars 4–7) ....

   (2)

FIRST VERSE (Bar 7 beat 4 to bar 13)

(d) What vocal technique is used by the singer on the words *away, afraid* and *die*?

   ....

   (1)

(e) How is the word *love* emphasised in the vocal line?

   ....

   (1)

(f) Name **two** instruments that accompany the singer in the verse.

   Instrument 1 ....

   Instrument 2 ....

   (2)

(Total for Question 6 = 8 marks)

Mark Scheme

Buckley	*Grace*	Introduction and first verse	CD track 14	

Question number	Correct answer	Mark
6(a)	**B** Bars 1 to 3 are in no clear key whereas bars 4 to 7 are in D major	1

Question number	Correct answer	Mark
6(b)	Sequence (ascending)	1

Question number	Correct answer	Mark
6(c)	1) Plucking/picking 2) Strumming	2

Question number	Correct answer	Mark
6(d)	Any **one** of: • Portamento • Glissando • Sliding • Fall off	1

Question number	Correct answer	Mark
6(e)	Any **one** of: • Melisma • Several notes set to one syllable • Descending scale	1

Question number	Correct answer	Mark
6(f)	Any **two** of: • Electric guitar • Acoustic guitar • Bass guitar • Drum kit/Toms	2

Area of Study 4
Rag Desh

7 Listen to the following two extracts featuring part of gat sections from different versions of Rag Desh, which will be played **three** times each.

(a) Apart from the instruments and/or voices, identify **one** difference between the two extracts.

Difference ....

(1)

(b) Name **two** of the instruments heard in **each** of the extracts.

EXTRACT 1	EXTRACT 2

(4)

(c) Name **three** other sections commonly found in a complete rag performance.

1 ....

2 ....

3 ....

(3)

(Total for Question 7 = 8 marks)

Mark Scheme

Rag Desh	Extract 1: Rag Desh as performed by Anoushka Shankar Extract 2: Slow gat in rupak tal performed by Steve Gorn and Benjy Wertheimer		CD track 15	

Question number	Correct answer	Mark
7(a)	Any **one** of: • First extract is faster than second • They use different tala patterns	1

Question number	Correct answer		Mark
7(b)	EXTRACT 1	EXTRACT 2	4
	• Sitar • Tabla	Any **two** of: • Bansuri • Tambura • Tabla	

Question number	Correct answer	Mark
7(c)	• Alap/alaap • Jhor/jor • Jhalla	3

Area of Study 4
Koko: Yiri

8 Listen to the following extract from Yiri, which will be played **three** times.

(a) (i) Which instrument plays the opening seven-bar solo?

....

(1)

(ii) Describe the texture of this section of the music.

....

(1)

(iii) How would you describe the metre of this solo section?

....

(1)

(3)

(b) After the introduction, what is the interval between the two parts playing the melody? Put a cross in the correct box.

A Thirds ☒

B Fifths ☒

C Sixths ☒

D Octave ☒

(1)

(c) The drums enter towards the end of the extract playing a three-note ostinato pattern. Using quaver and semiquaver rhythms, write out the **three-note rhythm** on the single-line stave below.

_____

(3)

(d) Name the two types of drum played in the extract.

1 ....

2 ....

(2)

(Total for Question 8 = 9 marks)

Mark Scheme

Koko	Yiri	Anthology bars 1–17	CD track 16	

Question number	Correct answer	Mark
8(a)	(i) balafon/balaphon	1
	(ii) monophonic	1
	(iii) free/unmetred	1

Question number	Correct answer	Mark
8(b)	**D** Octave	1

Question number	Correct answer	Mark
8(c)	Quaver (1), semiquaver (1) and semiquaver (1). Must be in this order. Crotchet, quaver, quaver = 1 mark only	3

Question number	Correct answer	Mark
8(d)	• Talking drum (large or small) • Djembe	2

SECTION B

Answer EITHER Question 9 OR Question 10

If you answer Question 9 put a cross in this box ☒.

9 The following questions are about the first movement from Symphony No. 40 in G minor, K550 by Mozart.

(a) In which century was this symphony composed?

....

(1)

(b) What style is this piece of music written in?

....

(1)

(c) Comment on how Mozart uses the following musical elements in the 1st movement from Symphony No. 40 in G minor, K550.

- Melody

- Harmony and tonality

- Texture

- Structure

- Instrumentation

Remember to use correct **musical vocabulary** where appropriate.

(10)

....
....
....
....
....
....
....
....
....
....
....
....
....

Mark Scheme

Mozart	1st Movement of Symphony No. 40 in G minor	

Question number	Correct answer	Mark
9(a)	18th century	1

Question number	Correct answer	Mark
9(b)	Classical	1

Question number	Indicative content
9(c) QWC i–ii–iii	**Melody** • Well proportioned/balanced and graceful melody lines • Regular (periodic) phrases/4+4 bars • Contrasting melodies as first and second subjects • Motif of first subject developed in central section (development) • Any other valid point **Harmony and tonality** • Harmony is largely diatonic • Functional harmony/based on chords I, II, IV, V (V7) and VI • Some chromatic notes • Diminished 7th used as a chromatic chord • Perfect cadences define keys • Music modulates to related/unrelated keys (credit any mention of keys passed through in development section) • First subject in G minor • Second subject in relative major B flat • Second subject in recapitulation is in tonic (G minor) • Any other valid point **Cont. over**

(Total for Question 9 = 12 marks)

Question number	Indicative content
9(c) cont. **QWC** **i–ii–iii**	**Texture** • Main texture is homophonic • Some dialogue between strings and woodwind • Oboes and bassoons often provide harmonic filling • Doubling of parts • Use of octaves • Orchestral textures are varied throughout the movement • Any other valid point **Structure** • Sonata form • Exposition, development and recapitulation sections • Contrast of two subjects/themes • Bridge section between first and second subjects (for modulation) • Exposition often repeated • Ends with a coda • Any other valid point **Instrumentation** • Classical orchestra • Strings • Seven woodwind players of one flute, two oboes, two clarinets, two bassoons • Brass section is two horns (in B flat and G) • No trumpets or timpani used in this work • Any other valid point

If you answer Question 10 put a cross in this box ☒.

10 The following questions are about *Why does my heart feel so bad* by Moby.

(a) In which year was this track released?

....

(1)

(b) What type or genre of music has influenced this song ?

....

(1)

(c) Comment on how Moby uses the following musical elements in *Why does my heart feel so bad*

- Structure
- Melody
- Harmony (chords)
- Technology
- Instrumentation

Remember to use correct **musical vocabulary** where appropriate.

(10)

....

....

....

....

....

....

....

....

....

....

....

....

....

....

....

If you answer Question 10 put a cross in this box ☒.

Mark Scheme

Moby	*Why does my heart feel so bad*	

Question number	Correct answer	Acceptable answer	Mark
10(a)	1999	Plus or minus ten years	1

Question number	Correct answer	Mark
10(b)	Dance music	1

Question number	Indicative content
10(c) **QWC** **i–ii–iii**	**Structure** • Alternates A (verse) and B (chorus) sections/intro-verse/chorus/verse/chorus • Any other valid point **Melody** • Uses two vocal samples • Taken from a 1953 gospel choir • Melody in verse is male • Melody in chorus is female • Samples have not been 'cleaned up' • Any other valid point **Harmony (chords)** • Whole song based on two simple chord patterns • Only uses 6 chords • Piano intro and verse Am/Em/G/D • Chorus is C/Am/C/Am then F/C/F/C • Harmony is diatonic and simple (characteristic of dance music) • Any other valid point **cont. over**

Question number	Indicative content
10(c) cont. **QWC** **i–ii–iii**	**Technology** • Use of loops • Reverb on piano and vocals (Yamaha SPX990) • EQ • Telephone effect (EQ) • Delay (Yamaha SPX990)/echo • Use of a filer • Drum machine (Roland TR909) • Sequencer • Sampler (Akai S3200) • Synth/string pad sounds (Yamaha SY22 and SY85) • Bass synth (Roland Juno 106) • Technology considered old fashioned for 1999 but preferred by Moby • Any other valid point **Instrumentation** • Piano • Synthesizers • Drum machine • Synth pads • String pads • Vocal samples • Any other valid point

Mark Scheme for Questions 9(c) and 10(c)

Level	Mark	Descriptor
Level 0	0	No positive features can be identified in the response.
Level 1	1–2 **Limited** analysing and evaluating skills	• Little relevant information regarding the question and set work(s) is conveyed. • Knowledge of key features of the set work(s) will be limited and/or incorrectly applied. • Range of musical vocabulary is limited and/or is not used correctly. • The skills needed to produce effective writing will not normally be present and answer lacks both clarity and organisation. Frequent spelling, punctuation and grammar errors will be present.
Level 2	3–4 **Basic** analysing and evaluating skills	• Some relevant information regarding the question and set work(s) is conveyed but there will be major omissions. • Knowledge of key features of the set work(s) will be basic with only the most obvious of comments made. • Range of musical vocabulary is basic but mostly used correctly. • The skills needed to produce effective writing are likely to be limited and passages within the answer will lack both clarity and organisation. Frequent spelling, punctuation and/or grammar errors will be present.
Level 3	5–6 **Competent** analysing and evaluating skills	• Relevant information regarding the question and set work(s) is conveyed but there will still be some (mostly) minor omissions. • Knowledge of key features of the set work(s) will be competent, with an adequate range of knowledge displayed. • Range of musical vocabulary is quite broad and is mostly used correctly. • Most of the skills needed to produce effective writing will be present but there will be lapses in clarity and organisation. Some spelling, punctuation and grammar errors will be present.
Level 4	7–8 **Good** analysing and evaluating skills	• Relevant information regarding the question and set work(s) is conveyed and omissions will be minor. • Knowledge of key features of the set work(s) will be good, with both range and some depth of knowledge displayed. • Range of musical vocabulary is broad and is mostly used correctly. • The skills needed to produce convincing writing are mostly in place. Good clarity and organisation. Some spelling, punctuation and grammar errors will be found but overall the writing will be coherent.
Level 5	9–10 **Excellent** analysing and evaluating skills	• Relevant information regarding the set work(s) is conveyed and any omissions are negligible. • Knowledge of key features of the set work(s) will be excellent, with a wide range and depth of knowledge displayed. • Range of music vocabulary is extensive and any errors in usage are minor. • All the skills needed to produce convincing writing are in place. Excellent clarity and organisation. Very few spelling, punctuation and/or grammar errors will be found and they will not detract from the overall coherence.

SECTION A

Answer all questions in this section.

Some questions must be answered with a cross in a box ☒. If you change your mind about an answer, put a line through the box ☒ and then mark your new answer with a cross ☒.

Area of Study 1
G.F. Handel: *And the glory of the Lord* from Messiah, HWV56

1   Listen to the following extract, which will be played **two** times.

(a) What is the name given to the part played by the organ and cello throughout the extract?

....

(1)

(b) Apart from the organ and cello, name **two** instruments that feature in the music of the extract.

1 ....

2 ....

(2)

(c) Which describes the order in which the voices first sing *and all flesh shall see it together*? Put a cross in the correct box.

   A Bass followed by Soprano   ☒

   B Soprano followed by Bass   ☒

   C Tenor followed by Soprano   ☒

   D Alto followed by Tenor   ☒

(1)

(d) (i) Describe the melody line of *for the mouth of the Lord hath spoken it*.

....

....

(2)

(ii) How does Handel make these words stand out clearly in the music?

....

....

(2)

(e) From what type of large-scale work does this chorus come?

....

(1)

(Total for Question = 9 marks)

Mark Scheme

Handel	*And the glory of the Lord* from Messiah	Anthology bars 38–63	CD track 17	

Question number	Correct answer	Mark
1(a)	(Basso) continuo	1

Question number	Correct answer	Mark
1(b)	• Violin(s) • Viola(s)	2

Question number	Correct answer	Mark
1(c)	**D** Alto followed by Tenor	1

Question number	Correct answer	Mark
1(d)(i)	Any **two** of: • Lots of repeated notes/As • Melody has only two different notes/pitches/As and Bs • Syllabic	2
1(d)(ii)	Any **two** of: • Sung loudly/*forte*/*f* • The words are repeated several times • Continuo/organ and cello also double the bass part	2

Question number	Correct answer	Mark
1(e)	Oratorio	1

Area of Study 1
Mozart: 1ˢᵗ movement from Symphony No. 40 in G minor, K550

2 Listen to the following extract, which will be played **three** times.

(a) At the start of the extract, which three woodwind instruments play the motif?

1 ....

2 ....

3 ....

(3)

(b) Describe the dynamics in the extract as a whole. Make **two** points.

1 ....

2 ....

(2)

(c) The music in the coda is based on which theme? Put a cross in the correct box.

1ˢᵗ Subject   ☒

2ⁿᵈ Subject   ☒

(1)

(d) Complete the following about the last eight bars of the extract:

The whole orchestra plays loudly in a(n) .... texture and

the harmony is based only on chords I and .... The movement ends with

a .... cadence in .... minor.

(4)

(Total for Question 2 = 10 marks)

Mark Scheme

Mozart	1st Movement of Symphony No. 40 in G minor	Anthology bars 260–299	CD track 18	

Question number	Correct answer	Mark
2(a)	• Clarinet • Flute • Bassoon (in any order) One mark for each correct answer	3

Question number	Correct answer	Mark
2(b)	Any **two** of: • Much use of contrasting dynamics • Some use of dynamic shading (crescendos and diminuendos) • Starts quietly/*piano*/***p*** • Then loud (tutti/full orchestra), • Suddenly quiet again • Ends forte/loud (tutti/full orchestra)	2

Question number	Correct answer	Mark
2(c)	1st subject	1

Question number	Correct answer	Mark
2(d)	1) Homophonic/chordal 2) V/five 3) Perfect/full close/V–I 4) G minor/tonic	4

Area of Study 2
Arnold Schoenberg: *Peripetie* from Five Orchestral Pieces, Op. 16

3 Listen to the following extract, which will be played **three** times.

(a) What word describes the tonality of this music? Put a cross in the correct box.

    A Atonal ☒

    B Major ☒

    C Minor ☒

    D Modal ☒

                                                           (1)

(b) Listen to the extract. State **two** ways in which texture is used and two ways in which dynamics are used in the music.

Texture

1 ....

2 ....

                                                           (2)

Dynamics

1 ....

2 ....

                                                            (2)

(c) (i) The chord played by the full orchestra just before the end of the extract includes the notes C, D, E♭, F♯, G and G♯. What is the name of a chord made up of these notes?

      ....

                                                             (1)

(ii) What word describes this chord? Put a cross in the correct box.

      A Pianissimo ☒

      B Dissonant ☒

      C Pentatonic ☒

      D Consonant ☒

                                                              (1)

(d) Give **two musical** reasons why you like or dislike this piece of music.

1 ....

2 ....

                                                             (2)

(Total for Question = 9 marks)

Mark Scheme

Schoenberg	*Peripetie* from Five Orchestral Pieces, Op.16	Anthology bars 59–66	CD track 19	

Question number	Correct answer	Mark
3(a)	**A** Atonal	1

Question number	Correct answer	Mark
3(b)	**Texture** Any **two** of: • Starts with just clarinet (1) and strings (1) • Thin/sparse texture • Quickly builds up with new parts coming in • Full orchestra plays a loud chord (1) just before the end (1) **Dynamics** Any **two** of: • Starts very quietly/*pianissimo*/***pp*** (1) • Gets louder (1)/crescendos (1) quickly (1) • Reaches very loud/*fortissimo*/***ff*** (1) then • Suddenly then dims/gets softer (1) • Ends ***ppp***/very very soft	4

Question number	Correct answer	Mark
3(c)(i)	Hexachord	1
3(c)(ii)	**B** Dissonant	1

Question number	Acceptable answers	Mark
3(d)	Any valid **musical** answers e.g. no clear melody/no sense of key/complex rhythms	2

Area of Study 2
Bernstein: *Something's coming* from West Side Story

4 Listen to the following extract, which will be played **five** times.

(a) Look at the following melody, which is heard at the beginning of the extract. Fill in the missing notes in bars 4–6. The rhythm is given above the stave.

Come on, some-thing, come on in. ___ Don't be shy, meet a guy ___

(4)

(b) Complete the following table, describing the melody line at the given lyrics. An example is shown below.

LYRICS	MUSIC
Come on, something, come on in, don't be shy, meet a guy, pull up a chair.	Lots of repeated and accented crotchet notes. Melody only uses four pitches. It is sung loudly in the middle of the vocal range
The air is humming, and something great is coming.	

(2)

(c) Describe how the song ends on the words *maybe tonight*.

....

(1)

(d) What is the overall mood of this song?

....

(1)

(Total for Question = 8 marks)

Mark Scheme

Bernstein	*Something's coming* from West Side Story	Anthology bars 118–158	CD track 20	

Question number	Correct answer	Mark
4(a)	One mark for each correct pitch	4

Question number	Correct answer	Mark
4(b)	Any **two** of: • High pitch/high register • Wide range of notes/7th • Long/sustained/held notes • Tied notes over the bar lines • Triplet rhythms • Cross rhythms • Sung quietly • Legato/cantabile style	2

Question number	Correct answer	Mark
4(c)	Any **one** of: • Ends on a long held note/C natural • Music fades out/diminuendo • No cadence	1

Question number	Correct answer	Mark
4(d)	Any **one** of: • excited • feeling of anticipation/expectation • nervous energy • optimistic • positive • upbeat	1

Area of Study 3
Moby: *Why does my heart feel so bad* from the album Play

5   Listen to the following extracts which will be played **three** times.

(a) What is the tempo of the song? Put a cross in the correct box.

A   98 bpm   ☒

B   118 bpm   ☒

C   138 bpm   ☒

D   158 bpm   ☒

(1)

(b) Identify **three** differences and **three** similarities between the two extracts.

Differences

1 ....

2 ....

3 ....

Similarities

1 ....

2 ....

3 ....

(6)

(c) When was the album 'Play' released? Put a cross in the correct box.

A   1979   ☒

B   1989   ☒

C   1999   ☒

D   2009   ☒

(1)

(Total for Question 5 = 8 marks)

Mark Scheme

Moby	*Why does my heart feel so bad*	**Sections Bx1 and Bx2**	**CD track 21**	

Question number	Correct answer	Mark
5(a)	**A** 98 bpm	1

Question number	Correct answer	Mark
5(b)	**DIFFERENCES** Any **three** of: • Instrumentation (must be specific) – no drums (1), bass (1) or piano (1) in second extract • Second extract has more reverb (1) and delay (1) on vocals • Vocals are quieter in the second extract • More sustained chordal accompaniment in the second extract **SIMILARITIES** Any **three** of: • Same key • Same time signature • Same tempo • Same vocal sample/same lyrics • Both are taken from the chorus • Both include the synth string pad	6

Question number	Correct answer	Mark
5(c)	**C** 1999	1

Area of Study 3
Miles Davis: *All blues* from the album Kind of Blue

6 Listen to the following extract which will be played **three** times.

(a) What instrument is playing the solo line? Put a cross in the correct box.

    A Clarinet ☒

    B String Bass ☒

    C Tenor Saxophone ☒

    D Trumpet ☒

(1)

(b) The piano is 'comping' underneath the solo. Explain what is meant by the term 'comping'.

....

....

(2)

(c) What standard chord sequence has been adapted for use in *All blues*?

....

(1)

(d) How many choruses are played in the extract?

....

(1)

(e) Describe the solo part, using musical vocabulary where appropriate.

....

....

....

(3)

(Total for Question 6 = 8 marks)

Mark Scheme

Miles Davis	*All blues*	Coltrane solo	CD track 22	

Question number	Correct answer	Mark
6(a)	**C** Tenor Saxophone	1

Question number	Correct answer	Mark
6(b)	Any **two** of: • Accompanying/providing a backing for the soloist to improvise over • Improvising on the chords • Playing rhythmic/chordal fills • Any other valid point	2

Question number	Correct answer	Mark
6(c)	12-bar blues	1

Question number	Correct answer	Mark
6(d)	Two	1

Question number	Correct answer	Mark
6(e)	Any **three** of: • Improvised • Florid/highly intricate/ornamented • Sometimes chromatic • Modal • Virtuosic • Makes much use of scale and arpeggio figures • Often syncopated • Any other valid point	3

Area of Study 4
Capercaillie: *Chuir m'athair mise dhan taigh charraideach (the Skye Waulking Song)* from the album **Nadurra**

7 Listen to the following extract, which will be played **three** times.

(a) Name **two** instruments playing the solo line.

1 ....

2 ....

(2)

(b) Describe what happens in the texture of the extract.

....

....

....

(2)

(c) What is the tonality of the extract? Put a cross in the correct box.

    A   Atonal   ☒

    B   Major   ☒

    C   Minor   ☒

    D   Pentatonic   ☒

(1)

(d) What is the time signature of the extract? Put a cross in the correct box.

    A   2/4   ☒

    B   5/4   ☒

    C   9/8   ☒

    D   12/8   ☒

(1)

(e) What section of the song is the extract taken from?

....

(1)

(f) How is folk music normally learned?

....

(1)

(Total for Question 7 = 8 marks)

Mark Scheme

Capercaillie	Chuir m'athair mise dhan taigh charraideach (the Skye Waulking Song)	Instrumental	CD track 23	

Question number	Correct answer	Mark
7(a)	Any **two** of: • Uilleann pipes • Fiddle • Accordion	2

Question number	Correct answer	Mark
7(b)	Any **two** of: • Occasionally heterophonic • Most of the extract has a dense texture • Staying consistent throughout • Until the very end when it thins out • To just vocals and drum kit • The instruments interweave • Contrapuntal	2

Question number	Correct answer	Mark
7(c)	**B** Major	1

Question number	Correct answer	Mark
7(d)	**D** 12/8	1

Question number	Correct answer	Acceptable answer	Mark
7(e)	Any **one** of: • Instrumental • Solo	Middle 8	1

Question number	Correct answer	Mark
7(f)	Any **one** of: • Oral tradition • Passed on by copying other musicians • By ear/rote	1

Area of Study 4
Koko: *Yiri*

8 Listen to the following extract, which will be played **three** times.

(a) Which of the following best describes the rhythm played by the drums? Put a cross in the correct box.

A ☒

B ☒

C ☒

D ☒

(1)

(b) Complete the sentences by using the words below. You may use words once, more than once or not at all.

Talking drums   Djembes   Balafons   Vocals   Mbiras

(i) At the beginning of the extract a solo is played by the ....

(ii) Throughout the extract the .... play an ostinato.

(iii) At the end of the extract there is call and response between two parts.

The .... call and the .... respond.

(4)

(c) What part of the world does the music come from?

....

(1)

(d) Name **two** rhythmic devices commonly used in music from this part of the world.

1 ....

2 ....

(2)

(Total for Question 8 = 8 marks)

Mark Scheme

Koko	Yiri	Third section	CD track 24	

Question number	Correct answer	Mark
8(a)	**A**	1

Question number	Correct answer	Mark
8(b)(i)	Balafons	1
8(b)(ii)	Any **one** of: • Balafons • Djembes • Talking drums	1
8(b)(iii)	The **vocals** call and the **balafons** respond.	2

Question number	Correct answer	Mark
8(c)	(West) Africa/Burkina Faso	1

Question number	Correct answer	Mark
8(d)	Any **two** of: • Syncopation • Cross-rhythms • Polyrhythms • Rhythmic ostinati	2

SECTION B

Answer EITHER Question 9 OR Question 10

If you answer Question 9 put a cross in this box ☒.

9 The following questions are about the *3rd movement (fast)* from Electric Counterpoint by Reich.

(a) How many guitar parts is this piece written for?

....

(1)

(b) What is the style of this piece of music?

....

(1)

(c) Comment on how Reich uses the following musical elements in *3rd movement (fast)* from Electric Counterpoint

- Melody

- Tonality

- Texture

- Structure

- Rhythm

Remember to use correct **musical vocabulary** where appropriate.

(10)

....
....
....
....
....
....
....
....
....
....
....
....
....
....

Mark Scheme

Reich	Electric Counterpoint	

Question number	Correct answer	Mark
9(a)	Ten	1

Question number	Correct answer	Mark
9(b)	Minimalism	1

Question number	Indicative content
9(c) QWC i–ii–iii	**Melody** • Melodies are made up of motifs/cells • They are repeated/looped/ostinati • Live guitar plays the resultant melody • Interlocking melodies • Motifs grow slowly/metamorphosis through note addition • Four-part guitar canon • New idea (bar 36) strummed chords • Any other valid point **Tonality** • Opening is ambiguous/bars 1–32 • Bass (bar 33) defines key as E minor • Frequent changes between E minor and C minor (bar 74) • The music has no D sharps so can be regarded as modal • Mode = Aeolian transposed to E/E Aeolian • Any other valid point <div align="right">**cont. over**</div>

(Total for Question 9 = 12 marks)

Question number	Indicative content
9(c) cont. **QWC** **i–ii–iii**	**Texture** • Main texture is contrapuntal • Broken chords • Texture built up in layers • Starts with just one part/guitar 1, then live guitar • Then guitars 2–4 • Followed by bass guitars 1 and 2 • Then guitars 5–7 • Once all parts in, texture is fairly constant/constantly repeating patterns • Use of interweaving/interlocking rhythms • Texture thins out towards the end of piece • Guitars 5–7 drop out • Basses fade away at end • Any other valid point **Structure** • Two main sections • Followed by a coda • Could be described as ternary form • Main sections divided into four smaller sections • Sections defined by changes in key and texture • Any other valid point **Rhythm** • Changes in metre between 3/2 and 12/8 in section B • Rhythmically complex with much repetition • Rhythmic counterpoint • Displaced accents/metrical displacement • Any other valid point

If you answer Question 10 put a cross in this box ☒.

10 The following questions are about *Mhara janam maran* (Rag Desh) as performed by Chiranji Lal Tanwar (voice).

(a) How is this type of music learned?

....

(1)

(b) Which section of this performance features the 'fixed composition'?

....

(1)

(c) Comment on how the following musical elements are used in this performance of Rag Desh.

- Structure
- Melody
- Rhythm
- Dynamics
- Instrumentation

Remember to use correct **musical vocabulary** where appropriate.

(10)

....
....
....
....
....
....
....
....
....
....
....
....
....
....
....

Mark Scheme

Chiranji Lal Tanwar	*Mhara janam maran* (Rag Desh)	

Question number	Correct answer	Mark
10(a)	Any **one** of: • Oral tradition • By rote • By copying the guru	1

Question number	Correct answer	Acceptable answer	Mark
10(b)	Bhajan	Gat	1

Question number	Indicative content
10(c) **QWC** **i–ii–iii**	**Structure** • Two main sections – alap and bhajan • Alap starts with a short introduction on the sarangi • Continues with some improvisation by the singer • The bhajan starts when the tabla enter • There are 3 'verses' in the bhajan • Interspersed with instrumental solos and sung 'choruses' • The piece ends with a short tihai • Any other valid point **Melody** • The melody is based on the notes of Rag Desh • Rag has more notes descending than ascending/5 notes ascending, 7 notes descending • The melody is ornamented (whether sung or played), with much melisma and meend • Most of the intervals are by step – the melody is mostly conjunct • Flowing • Any other valid point **Rhythm** • Tal/Keherwa Tal used in this performance • 8-beat tal (2+2+2+2) • A short tihai occurs at the end of the piece • The alap is in free time • The bhajan is where the tal can be heard • Any other valid point

Question number	Indicative content
10(c) cont. **QWC** **i–ii–iii**	**Dynamics** • The rag begins very quietly • There is a crescendo as the instruments and vocals enter • The dynamics increase when the tabla and other percussion enter for the bhajan • The dynamics stay at a similar level throughout • Other than some sudden bursts from the instruments and percussion accents • Any other valid point **Instrumentation** • Voice • Sarangi • Sarod • Pakhawaj • Cymbals • Tabla • Any other valid point

78   Edexcel GCSE in Music   Practice Listening Paper C: mark scheme   © Pearson Education 201

Mark Scheme for Questions 9(c) and 10(c)

Level	Mark	Descriptor
Level 0	0	No positive features can be identified in the response.
Level 1	1–2 **Limited** analysing and evaluating skills	• Little relevant information regarding the question and set work(s) is conveyed. • Knowledge of key features of the set work(s) will be limited and/or incorrectly applied. • Range of musical vocabulary is limited and/or is not used correctly. • The skills needed to produce effective writing will not normally be present and answer lacks both clarity and organisation. Frequent spelling, punctuation and grammar errors will be present.
Level 2	3–4 **Basic** analysing and evaluating skills	• Some relevant information regarding the question and set work(s) is conveyed but there will be major omissions. • Knowledge of key features of the set work(s) will be basic with only the most obvious of comments made. • Range of musical vocabulary is basic but mostly used correctly. • The skills needed to produce effective writing are likely to be limited and passages within the answer will lack both clarity and organisation. Frequent spelling, punctuation and/or grammar errors will be present.
Level 3	5–6 **Competent** analysing and evaluating skills	• Relevant information regarding the question and set work(s) is conveyed but there will still be some (mostly) minor omissions. • Knowledge of key features of the set work(s) will be competent, with an adequate range of knowledge displayed. • Range of musical vocabulary is quite broad and is mostly used correctly. • Most of the skills needed to produce effective writing will be present but there will be lapses in clarity and organisation. Some spelling, punctuation and grammar errors will be present.
Level 4	7–8 **Good** analysing and evaluating skills	• Relevant information regarding the question and set work(s) is conveyed and omissions will be minor. • Knowledge of key features of the set work(s) will be good, with both range and some depth of knowledge displayed. • Range of musical vocabulary is broad and is mostly used correctly. • The skills needed to produce convincing writing are mostly in place. Good clarity and organisation. Some spelling, punctuation and grammar errors will be found but overall the writing will be coherent.
Level 5	9–10 **Excellent** analysing and evaluating skills	• Relevant information regarding the set work(s) is conveyed and any omissions are negligible. • Knowledge of key features of the set work(s) will be excellent, with a wide range and depth of knowledge displayed. • Range of music vocabulary is extensive and any errors in usage are minor. • All the skills needed to produce convincing writing are in place. Excellent clarity and organisation. Very few spelling, punctuation and/or grammar errors will be found and they will not detract from the overall coherence.

CD acknowledgements

Tracks 1 and 18: Wolfgang Amadeus Mozart: 1st movement from Symphony No. 40 in G minor, K550
Capella Istropolitana, conducted by Barry Wordsworth
Licensed courtesy of Naxos Rights International Ltd

Tracks 2 and 10: Fryderyk Chopin: Prelude, Op. 28 No. 15 ("Raindrop")
Idil Biret (piano)
Licensed courtesy of Naxos Rights International Ltd

Tracks 3 and 12: Steve Reich: 3rd movement from Electric Counterpoint
Pat Metheney (guitar)
Licensed courtesy of Nonesuch Records/Warner Music UK

Tracks 4 and 19: Arnold Schoenberg: *Peripetie* from Five Pieces for Orchestra, Op. 16
London Symphony Orchestra, conducted by Robert Craft
Licensed courtesy of Naxos Rights International Ltd

Tracks 5 and 14: Jeff Buckley: *Grace* from the album Grace
Jeff Buckley (voice, guitars, keyboards), Mick Grondahl (bass), Matt Johnson (drums), Gary Lucas (magicalguitarness)
Courtesy of Sony Music Entertainment UK Ltd
Licensed by Sony Music Commercial Markets UK

Tracks 6 and 21: Moby: *Why does my heart feel so bad* from the album Play
Moby, Shining Light Gospel Choir (vocals)
Licensed courtesy of Mute Records Limited

Tracks 7 and 23: Traditional, arranged Capercaillie: *Chuir m'athair mise dhan taigh charraideach (the Skye Waulking Song)* from the album Nàdurra
Capercaillie
Capercaillie/Survival Records
Taken from the CD Nadurra SURCD 025
www.capercaillie.co.uk

Track 8: Alok Bhatt: *Mhara janam maran – Raga Desh* from the album Mewar Ree Mira: Devotional songs of Mirabai
Chiranji Lal Tanwar (voice), Ramzan Khan (sarangi), Kishore Dhandara (sarangi), Amit Goswami (sarod), Jaffar Mohamad (tabla), Ashwini Sharma (flute), Vijay Dagga (dholak) Praveen Arya (pakhawaj), Satish Sharma (cymbals)
Courtesy of Navras Records Limited
www.navrasrecords.com

Tracks 9 and 17: George Frideric Handel: *And the glory of the Lord* from Messiah, HWV56
Scholars Baroque Ensemble
Licensed courtesy of Naxos Rights International Ltd

Tracks 11 and 20: Leonard Bernstein: *Something's coming* from West Side Story
Larry Kert (voice)
From The Original Broadway Cast Recording of *West Side Story*
Courtesy of Sony Music Entertainment UK Ltd
Licensed by Sony Music Commercial Markets UK

Tracks 13 and 22: Miles Davis: *All blues* from the album Kind of Blue
Miles Davis (trumpet), Julian "Cannonball" Adderley (alto saxophone), John Coltrane (tenor saxophone), Bill Evans (piano), Paul Chambers (bass), Jimmy Cobb (drums)
Courtesy of Sony Music Entertainment UK Ltd
Licensed by Sony Music Commercial Markets UK

Track 15: Extract 1 – Ravi Shankar: *Raga Desh* from the album Anoushka Shankar Live at Carnegie Hall
Anoushka Shankar (sitar), Bikram Ghosh (tabla), Tanmoy Bose (tabla), Ajay Sharma (tanpura), Barry Phillips (tanpura) Anthony Karasek (tanpura), Natasha Ahmad (tanpura)
Licensed courtesy of EMI Records Limited

Extract 2 – Steve Gorn and Benjy Wertheimer: *Raga Desh Part Two (Gat in Rupak Tal)* from the album Priyagītah: The Nightingale
Steve Gorn (bansuri bamboo flute, clarinet), Benjy Wertheimer (esraj, tabla, vocals, keyboards), David Michael (zither) Michael Stirling (tamboura)
Licensed courtesy of Steve Gorn, Benjy Wertheimer and Shantala Music

Tracks 16 and 24: Madou Koné: *Yiri* from the album Burkina Faso: Balafons et tambours
Written by Madou Koné
Performed by Koko
Licensed courtesy of Sunset-France